BOOK ANALYSIS

By Tara Dorrell

The Satanic Verses

BY SALMAN RUSHDIE

BrightSummaries.com

SALMAN RUSHDIE

BRITISH INDIAN WRITER

- **Born in Bombay, British India in 1947.**
- **Notable works:**
  - *Midnight's Children* (1981), novel
  - *Joseph Anton: A Memoir* (2012), autobiography
  - *Two Years, Eight Months and Twenty-Eight Nights* (2015), novel

Born in Bombay (now Mumbai), India in 1947, Salman Rushdie was educated at Rugby School in Warwickshire, England, before studying history at King's College Cambridge. His first novel was published in 1975, but it was not until his second, *Midnight's Children,* that he began to receive literary attention. Influenced by James Joyce (Irish writer, 1882-1941), Gabriel García Márquez (Colombian writer, 1927-2014) and J. G. Ballard (English writer, 1930-2009), his work often contains elements of magic realism, as well as a frame narrative to tell parallel stories. His novels are noted for being highly satirical and have been labelled as "comic epics".

The Satanic Verses is unquestionably Rushdie's most famous work, as the book sparked controversy a few months after its initial publication, in 1989. Its references to Islam were seen by some as blasphemous, and in February of that year a fatwa was issued against Rushdie by Ayatollah Ruhollah Khomeini (1902-1989), the then Supreme Leader of Iran. It called for the death of Rushdie and his publishers, and a bounty was placed on him. Despite this, in 2007 the UK knighted him for services to literature.

THE SATANIC VERSES

A FANTASTICAL JOURNEY BETWEEN THE MODERN DAY AND REALMS OF OLD

- **Genre:** magical realist novel
- **Reference edition:** Rushdie, S. (1988) *The Satanic Verses*. London: Penguin Random House.
- **1st edition:** 1988
- **Themes:** heaven, hell, alienation, migration, identity, metamorphosis, belief, magic realism, rebirth

The Satanic Verses uses a frame narrative to combine several stories filled with magic realism (a genre of literature combining magical or fantastical elements with a realistic narrative), connecting them through time and space. Partially inspired by the life of the Prophet Muhammed, it follows the lives of two men after they fall out of a hijacked aeroplane only to take on the characteristics of the angel Gabriel and the devil.

Although the reception it received from critics was generally quite favourable, the book sparked outrage among the Muslim community, leading to book burnings and protests, and a ban on the novel in over ten countries around the world. Sales of *The Satanic Verses* massively increased following the fatwa issued against Rushdie, even though several people died in protests regarding the book, while his publishers and translators were individually targeted.

SUMMARY

TWO MEN AND A PROPHET

The Satanic Verses opens with the two protagonists, Gibreel Farishta and Saladin Chamcha, falling from a hijacked plane above the English Channel. Rushdie uses a frame narrative to tell multiple stories over the course of the novel explaining both their situation and the bizarre events that follow them throughout. Saladin had been on the plane after a trip to Bombay to see his father, where the two had come to blows, while Gibreel was flying to England to find a girl called Alleluia Cone, with whom he had had a glorious three-day-long affair. One of the hijackers who takes control of the plane, a female suicide bomber, blows the aircraft up, thus killing herself and trying to take everyone with her.

As they fall through the sky, Gibreel has a number of visions which later continue to follow him through his life. One is of Mahound, a name synonymous with Muhammed, the

Islamic prophet. Described as a "business-man", he enters the city of Jahilia, where he begins to spread the word of Allah, relying on his visions of an angel for information – not knowing that this angel is actually the human Gibreel, who slips in and out of the visions and appears to have little control over what he can do. Mahound is attempting to convert the city, despite the resentment of the people. The city's leader, Abu Simbel, offers Mahound the conversion of all the citizens, should three of the people's old goddesses be included in the worship. Knowing how this would help him and his followers in the long run, Mahound retires to consult with Gibreel. On the day of the city's famous poetry competition, he writes out a series of verses acknowledging the three goddesses, all while in a trance. The people all accept the new religion, but Mahound later retracts his verses, calling them "satanic" and claiming he was tricked into writing them by Shaitan (Satan), only to later be shown his error by Gibreel – unaware that his two interactions were in fact both with the human Gibreel.

WHEN IN LONDON

In the real world, Gibreel and Saladin have landed outside the home of Rosa Diamond, an elderly lady who allows the pair to stay with her. Between falling from the plane and washing up on English shores, the two have taken on certain religious characteristics: Gibreel is encircled by a glowing halo, connecting him to the archangel Gabriel. Saladin, meanwhile, has two hornlike lumps sprouting from his forehead, linking him to the devil. While staying with Rosa, Saladin is arrested as an illegal immigrant, and Gibreel does nothing to stop his arrest. Saladin becomes increasingly goat-like in appearance and manner, his horns fully forming and his legs becoming hoofed and hairy. He manages to convince the police – who seem to shift and change appearance as much as he does – that he is a British citizen, and is eventually able to call his wife, Pamela. However, he is instead answered by his old schoolfriend, "jumpy" (p. 181) Jamshed Joshi, with whom his wife is having an affair. Joshi helps Saladin, and takes him to his friend Muhammed Sufyan, who allows him to stay above the Sufyan family's restaurant, the Shaandaar Café. Furious at how Gibreel abandoned him, Saladin is ultimately overcome with rage, and in his fury expels his devil-like features, so he once more appears human.

Gibreel, meanwhile, has headed to London in search of Alleluia Cone, mountain climber extraordinaire and his three-day lover. Managing to find her, he collapses outside her house whereupon another vision takes hold. This time he sees an Imam who opposes the Empress Ayesha. He forces Gibreel to fly him across the country and then fight the goddess Al-lat, who Gibreel defeats by pure luck. He then falls into a vision of Ayesha of Titlipur, an orphan who convinces an entire village to take a pilgrimage to Mecca, following her visions of an angel, who is once again only the human Gibreel. This is done, much to the consternation of Mirza Saeed Akhtar, whose wife, dying of cancer, follows regardless.

Gibreel begins to live with Ally, although their relationship is mostly centred on their sex life. Gibreel, whose behaviour has been becoming increasingly schizophrenic, becomes incensed at the thought of Ally being near any other man, regularly flying into vicious rages. After one of these outbursts, he has a vision of who he assumes to be

God, prompting him to go out and 'save London'. It is unclear if this really is God, or actually Shaitan. Gibreel fails miserably at his task and is eventually hit by a car belonging to a film producer called Mr Sisodia, who convinces him to re-enter the limelight. During Gibreel's grand and long-awaited re-entry into stardom at a huge party, he creates a heatwave in London then passes out, and we are shown another vision, again of Mahound, several years on. Having previously fled the city, he had later returned to take full control of it, enforcing strict laws that appear to not apply to him, and citing Gibreel as his authority when questioned.

AYESHA, AND THE RETURN TO INDIA

Saladin is now living with Joshi and Pamela, uncaring of their affair or the fact that Pamela is pregnant with Joshi's child. The trio are invited to a party by one of Saladin's old colleagues, where he sees Gibreel again for the first time. After spending time with Gibreel and Ally, he notes their toxic relationship and uses his skill as a voice actor to break apart their relationship with a series of anonymous calls that exacerbate Gibreel's jealousy. Later, the Shaandaar Café catches fire and

Saladin runs in in an attempt to save the Sufyans. Gibreel, who has realised Saladin is behind the phone calls, saves him regardless. While they are unconscious, we are given the final vision, of the outcome of Ayesha's pilgrimage. Many of the pilgrims had died during the journey, and several had lost their faith. Nevertheless, many more walk into the Arabic Sea behind Ayesha, who has told them the waters will part for them to reach Mecca. This does not happen, and everyone who walks into the water drowns.

Later, both Saladin and Gibreel return to Bombay, where the former reconciles with both his dying father and his Indian heritage, reconnecting with an Indian woman called Zeeny who wants him to embrace his roots. Gibreel has been attempting a series of films all based on his visions, but every single one has flopped. Ally is later found having fallen to her death from Gibreel's residence, a building aptly named "Everest". Mr Sisodia is found dead inside, and Gibreel later shows up at Saladin's home, a prime suspect for the two deaths. After attempting to convince Saladin of his innocence while justifying his jealousy, he puts a gun to his mouth and kills himself.

CHARACTER STUDY

GIBREEL FARISHTA

Gibreel Farishta is a sought-after Bollywood star, best known for his theological roles. He initially began work transporting tiffin carriers across Bombay, but is now one of the most favoured actors in the business. He is known for having relations with women left, right and centre, including his neighbour Rekha Merchant, who later commits suicide by jumping off of their tall apartment building, taking her children with her. His original name was Ismail Najmuddin, but he got the name 'Farishta' from his mother, who said he was "her personal angel" (p. 19), and "too damn sweet" (*ibid.*). He has always been interested in reincarnation and various religions, but had lost his faith after a close brush with death with an unknown illness. However, after falling from the hijacked plane he appears to have merged with the angel Gabriel, although the extent of his power is unclear – it is uncertain whether he is actually connected to the angel at all, or if his visions are the result of schizophrenia. It often seems that his halo is the only thing marking him as different from anyone else, although he does manage to create a heatwave across London at one point. Within his visions, he seems capable of very little and instead watches, helpless, while Mahound, Ayesha and the Imam choose to interpret his presence as best suits their needs.

Some of this inaction spreads into the 'real' world, when he watches unconcerned as Saladin is arrested and taken away. His pompous and arrogant nature takes a toll on his relationship with Ally, which is then heightened by the jealous fits he throws at the mere mention of another man's name. It is this that proves to be his downfall: although almost his entire life has been spent loving India and her deities, whether he was rich or poor, it is his love for a Western woman that causes both their deaths.

SALADIN CHAMCHA

Previously known as Salahuddin Chamchawala, Saladin changes his name when he moves to England, in an attempt to leave behind his cruel and overbearing father and the Indian world he represents. Saladin's name was the cause of some upset among Muslim readers, as it connected the devil to the Muslim defender against Christian Crusaders, also called Saladin. During the novel he comes to symbolise Shaitan, or Satan, gaining a goat-like appearance complete with horns and a tail and becoming increasingly inhuman in manner too. Born into a wealthy Indian family but continuously in conflict with his father throughout childhood and into adulthood, their relationship had only worsened after Saladin went to a boarding school in England. He later took on jobs as a voice actor in the UK, which he adores in spite of the racism, living there permanently and marrying an English belle called Pamela Lovelace. Saladin's love for Pamela comes from the connection she gives him to England, while the woman he ends up with, Zeeny, reconnects him to India.

He is something of an antithesis to Gibreel, although perhaps not to the extent the reader might expect, given the personas they take on. Throughout the novel Saladin suffers with his own personal demons of his heritage and family life, making his appearance all the more ironic. In spite of the elements of magic realism that pervade his life, his story is far easier to follow than Gibreel's, as it clearly takes him from India and back again and examines how he comes to love his homeland once more.

ALLELUIA CONE

Alleluia Cone is an English mountain climber and Gibreel's girlfriend for much of the novel. Nicknamed the "ice queen" (p. 33), Ally is recognisable by her pale skin and blonde-white hair, and her love of all things related to Mount Everest. Prior to meeting Gibreel, she had conquered the mountain, in spite of the agonising fallen arches of her feet that prevent her from climbing further. While upon Everest, she herself had visions of a solo mountaineer named Maurice Wilson, who talks to her. Ally meets Gibreel after his recovery from a near-fatal illness and consequent loss of faith, and it is because of her that he is on Flight AI-420, travelling to England to find her once more. When he is diagnosed with schizophrenia, Ally cares for Gibreel, who time and again finds himself turning up at her house, often unaware of how he arrived there. Despite their electric sex life, Gibreel's vicious jealousy takes its toll on Ally, and the pair are pushed apart by Saladin's cruel tampering with their relationship. Towards the end of the novel, she is found dead in Bombay, having been pushed by Gibreel from the top of his residence, ironically also called Everest.

PAMELA LOVELACE

Pamela Chamcha, née Lovelace, is Saladin's wife, who for him symbolises everything he loves about England. She is known for her loud and dominating voice, a voice that denotes "tweeds, headscarves, summer pudding" (p. 180), all things identifiably English. Disappointed in Saladin's inability to make her pregnant, she finds a new lover in Jamshed Joshi when she believes her husband to be dead. She turns to alcohol to cope with his death, in spite of their loveless marriage, but eventually becomes pregnant with Joshi's child instead. However, the two are killed in a fire towards the end of the novel.

AYESHA OF TITLIPUR

One of the many characters named Ayesha in the book, Ayesha of Titlipur is a prominent figure in several of Gibreel's visions. Although she is prone to fits and seizures, and when we first see her, she is eating butterflies, she is soon accepted as the village's prophetess bringing messages from the archangel Gibreel. She predicts the cancer of Mirza Saeed Akhtar's wife, and informs them that the entire village must go on a pilgrimage, on foot, to Mecca for her cure. She assures them that the Arabian Sea will part for them to reach Mecca. Faithful to a fault, almost all the villagers follow her into the sea, where they drown. Many Muslims believed it to be blasphemous to use the name of the Prophet Muhammed's wife, Ayesha, for a fanatical girl who causes so many deaths.

MAHOUND

One of the most controversial characters in *The Satanic Verses*, Mahound is another key character in Gibreel's visions. Portrayed as a businessman, he is based on the Prophet Muhammed, and much like Ayesha, supposedly brings messages from Gibreel to the sand city of Jahilia. The name "Mahound" supposedly comes from an old Christian term for the prophet, used in the Crusades to vilify him. In one of Gibreel's visions, Mahound is asked whether three pre-Islamic goddesses, Lat, Uzza and Manat, can be included in the worship of the religion he speaks of. Mahound consults with Gibreel and allows the goddesses to remain, knowing how it will aid his attempts to convert the people of Jahilia. However, he later rescinds this, claiming the verses he had written on the matter to be "satanic". He flees, but in a later vision returns to Jahilia as its conqueror, his new religion having been adopted by everyone there. The visions show Mahound's rule to be filled with rules and restrictions, leading many people to turn away from it, particularly when they see his apparent exemption from the same laws, suspiciously backed by the archangel Gibreel.

ANALYSIS

CONTROVERSY

The publication of *The Satanic Verses* led to a controversy surrounding the book among the Muslim community, also known as the Rushdie Controversy. Some Muslims saw the sub-plots about Mahound – a variation on the name of the Prophet Muhammed used in the past by Christian writers to vilify him – as blasphemous, and in 1988 Pakistan banned the book. Over ten countries, including India, Kenya and Singapore, banned it, and it was burned in demonstrations and protests across the UK, in February 1989, a protest of over 10 000 people in Islamabad, Pakistan, saw six people killed. In addition to the derogatory name Mahound, people also objected to his portrayal in the story, as well as the name 'Ayesha' for the girl who ends up killing an entire village, and the depiction of Muhammed's wives as prostitutes. There were also connections between Saladin Chamcha, the Muslim leader who fought against Christian Crusaders, and the devil.

In February 1989, the Supreme Leader of Iran at the time, Ayatollah Ruhollah Khomeini, issued a fatwa calling for Rushdie's death, and a bounty of up to $3 million was put on his head. In June 1989 Khomeini died, which means that the fatwa was technically never retracted, in spite of the conciliatory statement issued by Iran in 1998. In 2016, $600 000 was added to the fatwa by 40 Iranian media organisations run by the state.

Although Rushdie himself was placed under 24-hour police protection, his publishers and translators of The Satanic Verses also came under fire. In 1991 the novel's Japanese translator was stabbed to death, while the Italian translator was seriously injured in an attack in Milan. Two years later, the publisher in Norway was shot three times but managed to survive, while the Turkish translator was potentially the target of the Sivas Massacre in Turkey, which led to 37 deaths.

The publication of the book led to international incidents, heightening tensions between Muslim countries and the West. Several bookshops in America were firebombed for selling the novel, and in March 1989 Iran broke off diplomatic relations with the UK.

In spite of this, Rushdie was knighted in 2007 for his services to literature. There were several international protests against this and al-Qaeda condemned his knighthood. It has been questioned whether the London 7/7 bombings were linked to the knighthood, but it is still unclear.

METAMORPHOSIS

Salman Rushdie is known for his use of magic realism in his texts, and the genre has a clear presence in *The Satanic Verses*. Throughout the novel, we see several examples of metamorphosis, particularly in the characters – the most obvious of course being in Gibreel and Saladin. After he falls from the plane, Gibreel takes on the characteristics of the angel Gabriel, while Saladin becomes more similar to Shaitan, the devil. Saladin has the more distinct transformation out of the two, physically growing horns on his head, as well as hair on his legs and hoofed feet, much like a goat. His mannerisms become increasingly goat-like too, his appetite waning until all food tastes the same. Because of this, the reader expects him to take on the role of the antagonist, yet for the most part Saladin is rarely actively evil. His cruellest act is using his skills as a voice actor to create a rift between Gibreel and Ally, heightening the former's jealousy that eventually makes him kill his girlfriend. It must be noted that during his stay in the Sufyan family's household, the relationships among the other family members drastically break down, particularly after Saladin expels his devil-like characteristics from his body in a fit of rage. It is possible that once these attributes are no longer in him, they spread to those around him instead.

Gibreel, meanwhile, has little to show for his newfound angelic identity, save a glowing halo that comes and goes. He attempts to save London, piece by piece, but is haunted by the ghost of Rekha Merchant, a woman who had loved him but committed suicide, taking all her children with her. Gibreel's visions and erratic behaviour lead to a diagnosis of schizophrenia, making the reader wonder to what extent these bizarre happenings are real. No one takes any notice when Gibreel grows to tower over the city, and often his presence as an 'angel' only seems to be noticeable in his own visions, and nowhere else.

The city of Jahilia is also notable for how it metamorphoses. A twisting city of sand, its name is a reference to the state of Mecca prior to Islam, and is often translated as the "age of ignorance". As Jahilia itself seems to twist and transform, so too does it transform within Gibreel's visions, changing from a moving, polytheistic city to one forced to a standstill, under the monotheism that Mahound brings. Within the city we also see the transformation of the people, notably the 12 women in the brothel who take on the identities of the wives of Mahound, and later their personalities too.

INDIAN IDENTITY

Salman Rushdie was born in Bombay, in British India, and studied in the UK. His work clearly connects the two countries, and shows him to be a victim of British colonialism in India. Although born into a liberal Muslim family, Rushdie now identifies as an atheist. It is possible that his rejection of the religion is partially why the book came under so much fire for allegedly being anti-Islam.

Within the novel, Saladin is clearly torn between

his Indian roots and the country he wants so desperately to be a part of, England. Much like Rushdie, Saladin is also educated in the UK and seeks to become a part of it at a time when racism is very prevalent and prevents him from holding down a job, in spite of his family's high status in India. For Saladin, his journey is about accepting his Indian identity, and by the end of the novel he does, signified not only by his reconciliation with his father, but also by the rekindling of his relationship with a former girl-friend, Zeeny, as opposed to Pamela. Gibreel, on the other hand, is proud of how he has dragged himself up from nothing, and is full of contempt for "proper London" (p. 4), despite attempting to redeem it later on. Although seemingly firmly rooted in his Indian heritage, his decision to be in a relationship with an English woman is what eventually leads to both his and her downfall – quite literally.

The book also had a hand in forging how Muslim identity is perceived in the West. The strong backlash the novel received from Iran led to the disintegration of relations between Iran and the UK, which in turn led to an increase in condemnation of *The Satanic Verses* by other Western countries, for fear of how it would disrupt their own diplomatic relations.

FURTHER REFLECTION

SOME QUESTIONS TO THINK ABOUT...

- Why do you think Saladin is the protagonist who survives at the end of the novel, while Gibreel dies?
- What are your thoughts on the narrator – are they God, Shaitan, or a third, independent party?
- Compare the characters of Ally and Pamela.
- How do you think the backgrounds of Saladin and Gibreel affect the story?
- Discuss the importance of Gibreel's visions on the main narrative regarding him and Saladin – how do they change our reading of the novel?
- Do you believe *The Satanic Verses* can ever be read without reflection on the controversy that surrounded it? Should it be?
- Discuss the theme of alienation within the novel.
- How does the novel reflect the post-colonial concerns of both Britain and India?

- What are your thoughts on the public response to the novel? Given the subject matter, do you think it can be viewed as ironic?
- Do you believe *The Satanic Verses* challenges religious texts? Explain your answer.

We want to hear from you!
Leave a comment on your online library
and share your favourite books on social media!

FURTHER READING

REFERENCE EDITION

- Rushdie, S. (1988) *The Satanic Verses*. London: Penguin Random House.

REFERENCE STUDIES

- Malik, K. (2018) The Satanic Verses sowed the seeds of rifts that have grown ever wider. *The Guardian: Opinion*. [Online]. [Accessed 15 March 2019]. Available from: <https://www.theguardian.com/commentisfree/2018/sep/29/satanic-verses-sowed-seeds-of-rift-grown-ever-wider>
- Rushdie, S. (2012) The Disappeared: How the fatwa changed a writer's life. *The New Yorker*. [Online]. [Accessed 15 March 2019]. Available from: <https://www.newyorker.com/magazine/2012/09/17/the-disappeared>

MORE FROM BRIGHTSUMMARIES.COM

- Reading guide – *Midnight's Children* by Salman Rushdie.

www.brightsummaries.com

Ebook EAN: 9782808019385

Paperback EAN: 9782808019392

Legal Deposit: D/2019/12603/136

Cover: © Primento

Digital conception by Primento, the digital partner of publishers.

TM

£5.25

Written by Michael Heatley.
Edited by Melanie J Clayden.
Design and layout by Joanna Davies.

Published by
GRANDREAMS LIMITED
Jadwin House, 205/211 Kentish Town Road,
London NW5 2JU.

Printed in Italy.

All information correct at time of going to press.

CONTENTS

Gladiators and contenders have undergone considerable training. Do not attempt to imitate their actions or recreate Gladiators *events. Play safely.*

TM

How It

THE HISTORY OF A

The whole Gladiators phenomenon started way back in the days of the Roman Empire from 264BC to 325AD, when the all-powerful Emperors employed Gladiators to battle in the arena. Their name came from 'Gladius', the Latin for sword. Some were criminals, others slaves, and a few were even prisoners of war – but all battled to the bitter end for their Emperor's entertainment. His thumbs-up or thumbs-down would determine each Gladiator's fate depending on the kind of fight they put up. These days, thankfully, it's the Eliminator that sorts out the men from the boys…

Take a leap forward two thousand years, and the inspiration for the spectacle we now know as *Gladiators* can be traced back to one person – man mountain turned screen sensation Arnold Schwarzenegger! Born in Austria, the former bodybuilder became an all-American hero in 1987's futuristic film *The Running Man* when he played a convict who was pitted against some pretty tough opposition in a fictional game show.

All Began

LEGENDARY TV SHOW

His battles with the likes of Buzzsaw, Subzero, Dynamo and Fireball saw him make a name for himself – and Samuel Goldwyn Productions, a TV company based at Universal Studios, seized the opportunity to turn fiction into fact. Not with Arnie, of course, but the man (and woman) in the street!

The show *American Gladiators* soon vaulted up the ratings, pitting men and women against the modern day equivalent of Roman Gladiators. When London Weekend Television took on the show four years ago, producer Nigel Lythgoe took the decision to use athletes as his Gladiators rather than exclusively bodybuilders, as in the US series. The result was a more family-orientated show with Gladiators glamorous enough to be pin-ups as well as heroes…and Mr Lythgoe is now LWT's Head of Entertainment, so he clearly got it right!

So much so, that with 14.5 million viewers tuning in regularly, there's no way British *Gladiators* can be considered a baby brother to the US series. With three series 'in the can', *Gladiators* has become a TV institution. And that was confirmed when US Gladiator Jazz said, 'If I didn't know better, I'd have thought *Gladiators* started here in Britain – the fans are so loud.' High praise indeed…

It takes a day to record two British *Gladiators* shows – one in the afternoon, the other in the evening. In both cases, four hours of filming are edited down over a two day period to make the 51 minutes we enjoy on our screens. Ten cameras are supplemented by two more mounted on technocranes for those amazing high altitude shots.

All in all, a whole lot has changed since Roman days. And even Arnie, the prototype Gladiator of modern times, would surely think twice before pitting his brain and his brawn against the finest Britain has to offer.

JET

FAVOURITE EVENT
Pyramid – 'Agility and all-round fitness helped me with that…it's such good fun to do.'

LEAST FAVOURITE EVENT
Joust – 'I don't think many of the girls like Joust because it is such a fighting, pugilistic game. Duel is kind of the same.'

FAVOURITE SPORTS
Gymnastics

OFF DUTY INTERESTS
One of Jet's main interests is music. She plays both the flute and pan pipes, though her preferred listening material ranges from the classical Mozart through the soulful tones of Aretha Franklin to *Guns N' Roses*. She also enjoys cinema-going and learning languages.

BIRTHDATE 13 February 1970
BIRTHPLACE Teesside
STAR SIGN Aquarius
HEIGHT 5ft 7in
WEIGHT 9st 5lbs
STATISTICS 38-24-36

“I don't get aggressive at all in *Gladiators*. I do my best, and if my best is being aggressive then that's what I'll be, but I don't think I am. Lightning and I are really just little girls but we've got the guts to succeed.”

“I have not yet reached my full potential, fitness-wise. I would like to see what sort of Gladiator I would make when I'm really, really, really in shape!”

“I get very nervous although I never show it. Fortunately, my nervous reaction is to smile a lot, so when Jet's flying around the arena dancing doing gymnastics and smiling it means she's nervous! But if I'm not nervous I start to get worried because the adrenalin doesn't pump and I don't perform my best.”

BETCHA DIDN'T KNOW...

Jet retired from the British Olympic Gymnastic Squad at the age of 13 when she made the decision to concentrate on her dancing. Now, *Gladiators* gives her the best of both worlds!

HUNTER

BIRTHDATE 12 June 1973
BIRTHPLACE Beverley
STAR SIGN Gemini
HEIGHT 6ft 3in
WEIGHT 18st
STATISTICS Chest 51in, waist 33in, arm 19in, leg 28in

FAVOURITE EVENT The Wall – 'Because I love climbing, it's one of my favourite things now.'

LEAST FAVOURITE EVENT Joust – 'It's no fun to do, just because it's so hard.'

FAVOURITE SPORTS Bodybuilding, judo

OFF DUTY INTERESTS Hunter is certainly game for a laugh – his favourite TV programmes are those comedy classics *Blackadder* and *Red Dwarf*! He also enjoys eating out – big helpings! – and going to the cinema.

"I trained for Atlaspheres by pushing cars, my old Astra, in the dead of winter in a car park near where I live with my mate steering. I'd get people coming over and saying, "Need any help?" so I'd have to tell them, "No, I'm doing this for fun!""

"To be a Gladiator, you need to be fit in all areas – not just strong. You've got to be fast, use your body weight, run, skip, jump, hop, whatever…I recommend building up your body in all areas."

"Cobra and I went away to Zimbabwe, and there were several teams racing each other on rafts. It was quite frightening, there were a lot of injuries, it was quite a dangerous thing to do, but it was a great experience and we were still smiling at the end of it all."

BETCHA DIDN'T KNOW...

Behind Hunter's so-tough exterior lies a tender artistic talent! He used to attend art college as a youth, still sketches occasionally – and, word has it, his mum is an artist!

PANTHER

BIRTHDATE 14 October 1963
BIRTHPLACE Blyth
STAR SIGN Libra
HEIGHT 5ft 7in
WEIGHT 10st 7lbs
STATISTICS 37-24-36

FAVOURITE EVENT
Powerball

LEAST FAVOURITE EVENT
Tilt

FAVOURITE SPORTS
Skiing, martial arts, aerobics

OFF DUTY INTERESTS
Football fanatic Panther is mad about Newcastle United and their pocket-sized boss, Kevin Keegan. She also enjoys listening to soul music and watching *Brookside* ('I just love the accents!').

"I've started doing karate recently and if I keep it up I think I'm going to improve my attitude. Before, I was almost feeling sorry for the contenders...I want to get that out of my mind!"

"At the end of the day you've got to give credit to the contenders and realise just how good these people are. They've got great determination to do five events against different Gladiators – I think that's great."

"I can't stay away from the gym. To me, it's more a way of life than a hobby – and once I start something I put my mind to it and commit myself totally!"

BETCHA DIDN'T KNOW...

By chance, Panther was spotted by producer Nigel Lythgoe when she appeared on the *Noel Edmonds Show* to talk about health and fitness. She'd already picked up four amateur bodybuilding titles (Miss Great Britain, Miss Europe, Miss World and Miss Universe) and was about to earn a fifth title – Gladiator!

Behind the

Wanna be a contender? Here's how!

Ever wondered where the contenders who appear on *Gladiators* come from? Next time you're walking down the street or browsing in the shops, stop and think twice – you could be looking at one! They come from every walk of life, from yachtsmen to secretaries, dance teachers to firemen, and they come in their thousands. No fewer than 25,000 applications were received for the third series, more than twice the number who put their name forward for its predecessor.

Each and every one of those entries was treated seriously. All the details from 25,000 application forms – ranging from health and fitness to height and weight, occupation and interests – were keyed into LWT's computers, with the result that one in two of the applicants was invited to take a punishing physical test at one of eight centres nationwide.

The tasks that faced them were as follows:
Running 800 metres in two and a half minutes (three minutes for women) on a moving track.
Performing 10 straight arm chin-ups (five for women) while hanging from a beam, with just five seconds recovery time between each.
Crossing a horizontal ladder.
Climbing a 20-foot rope twice in a minute (once for women).

That weeds out the weeds – only about one in a hundred get through all four of those stages. Then comes a duel, in which survivors are

scenes...

matched with contenders of equal stature. On trial here are aggression and self-control – you have to be able to take punishment as well as hand it out! After that, it's down to an interview on video to discover the outgoing personalities…all of which results in 50 potential contenders, the people with that certain something that sets them apart from the rest.

And even if these don't make it through to the final 32 who'll battle it out on screen in front of nearly 15 million fans, they can puff out their chest with pride at having got through the toughest test in televised sport.

There's no single secret of success – preparations are as different as the contenders themselves. Take Phil Campbell, (pictured left), a contender in the third series, for instance. He spent a lot of time running on a shingle beach where he thought the shifting stones would simulate the Travelator.

Dean Pollen, who's a keen rugby player, increased his weight training, while Gladstone McKenzie, who plays American football, is certain experience of the Gridiron game gave him an advantage in Powerball. 'It's about being able to take a hit, go down, get back up and move again…it's all about going for it.'

Couldn't have put it better ourselves!

WOLF

FAVOURITE EVENT
Pyramid – 'It's a rough old game, plenty of rolling and tumbling and a lot of argy bargy. It's fantastic…'

LEAST FAVOURITE EVENT
Atlaspheres

FAVOURITE SPORTS
Snakeboarding

OFF DUTY INTERESTS
The bad guy of the *Gladiators* arena, Wolf's viewing preferences range from *Star Trek* to *Wayne's World*, while musically he's into the sounds of songstress Mariah Carey. He also likes to snowboard and skate.

BIRTHDATE 30 September 1952
BIRTHPLACE Bombay, India
STAR SIGN Libra
HEIGHT 6ft
WEIGHT 15st
STATISTICS Chest 48in, waist 30in, arm 18in

“If you see my good side, that's only because I've had a lapse in concentration. I look upon the contenders as cannon fodder. If I'm being nice to them, I'm patronising them.”

“*Gladiators* is the ultimate challenge. It tests people to the limits. You push yourself as hard as you can and yet it's still just so much fun. That's fantastic!”

“My main weakness is patience - I don't like the contenders and I can get very aggressive. I take every game seriously. I don't like losing – I'm out there to win!”

BETCHA DIDN'T KNOW...

Wolf's ambitions of movie stardom meant he had to give up playing football for Gillingham's reserves. He's since made his first big-screen appearance as a baddie in a sci-fi film.

FALCON

FAVOURITE EVENT
Powerball

LEAST FAVOURITE EVENT
Tilt – 'It gives so much advantage to the contender.'

FAVOURITE SPORTS
Netball

OFF DUTY INTERESTS
Even with such a hectic schedule, Falcon still finds the time and energy to help various charities, including the NSPCC, and regularly attends fund-raising events. And to relax? She enjoys reading, watching a movie, or just simply going for a walk.

BIRTHDATE 6 November 1963
BIRTHPLACE Brighton
STAR SIGN Scorpio
HEIGHT 5ft 7.5in
WEIGHT 10st 7lbs
STATISTICS 38-24-34

‘When you come off, or do badly, everyone's there to encourage you and advise you on where you went wrong and how you can improve. We make a great team!’

‘I usually work out five days a week and the others are rest days, which you need so your body can recuperate and recover. I make sure I get enough energy with my food in-between the workouts.’

‘I like getting fan mail from children asking advice about exercise because they're interested in doing sport. All of us are role models and to be able to help them is really good...but a stamped addressed envelope is a great help!’

BETCHA DIDN'T KNOW...

Falcon has a ten-year-old son Adam, who never misses a show on television and watches it time and again on video. His fave Gladiator? Not Mum, sad to say – but Wolf!

The New Games

The producers of *Gladiators* never rest in their search to give viewers even more of what they want. So when they added four events to make 17 from which to choose, they didn't just make each show unique in itself – they multiplied the challenges for contender and Gladiator alike.

'You've got so many games to choose from now,' growls Wolf sullenly, 'even we don't know what's going to happen!'

Many new ideas are submitted to LWT, who vet each thoroughly. It takes between 12 and 15 weeks to work up an idea from the drawing board to test level: this includes costing out construction and sometimes even making a working model.

Even Gladiators have to train for new events. They are given a week to familiarise themselves with the new games before the contenders arrive on the scene, and are put through their paces by Olympic athlete Derek Redmond. Once the Gladiators have shown their prowess, producer Nigel Lythgoe can choose the men (and women) for the job – some Gladiators will be more suitable than others. So let's put the four new games under the spotlight...

POLE-AXE

Four more challenges to test the most courageous contender – plus our tips to topple 'em!

Even the Gladiators were wary of this metallic 40-foot pole which revolves as you climb and whose rungs sneakily retract the moment your opponent reaches the top to hit their button! The Gladiators started by climbing halfway up and falling off 'properly', on their backs. Once they'd mastered the art of falling from the very top, then the pole finally started revolving.

Some games favour contenders or Gladiators – but on Pole-Axe each has an equal chance. As Hunter says though, 'You have to be single-minded, because if you stop to think about what you're doing it slows you down.'

With her experience of pole-vaulting, Zodiac had a lot to live up to on Pole-Axe. 'The adrenalin rush is unlike everything else,' she admits, although she reminds us that '40 feet is quite a bit different from 14 feet, which is the height I jump.' Even so, she's come to terms with flying through the air with the greatest of ease – and it's significant this was the game the American Gladiators liked least on their first visit to the National Indoor Arena!

Supertip: Count how many rungs you have to climb before you get to the button – that can knock up to two seconds off your time…

PYRAMID

A great favourite with viewers, this is the one where contenders try to reach the summit and set off the fireworks – providing, that is, they can escape the clutches of those two guardian Gladiators! Plenty of spectacular falling and rolling on show here, with the odds favouring the Gladiators because, as Zodiac admits, when they grab their opponent for the long tumble down they'll most likely land on top! After they've done that, the Gladiators are supposed to return to the second step, and are not – repeat not – allowed to hold their opponents down.

Each step of the 25-foot structure is two feet high and, though it's been described as a bouncy castle for adults, the Pyramid is a truly awe-inspiring experience. Even Panther confesses to 'screaming all the way down from the top to the bottom the first time.'

Supertip: Try to outrun the guarding Gladiator and win by sheer speed – few contenders have succeeded by aiming straight for their opponent and dislodging them.

PURSUIT

A combination of zig-zagging a balance beam, a net trap that clings like quicksand, an up-and-over wall and a rope bridge – this is a souped-up version of the obstacle course well known from school sports days everywhere. What's more, it offers plenty of scope for shady tricks…as Wolf's shown by taking a strictly illegal shortcut or two! If everyone plays fair, though, it's a scientific test of strength, balance and speed – so the bulkier male Gladiators are unlikely to shine here.

The race usually lasts little longer than a minute, but is guaranteed to set the pulse rate soaring and the heart pumping – and that's just the spectators! Contenders enjoy a mere three second head start, and if they finish without being tagged by their pursuer they win ten and five points for first and second places. It's all fast, furious and fun!

Supertip: In the netting, just take a running jump and then leap out again, because there's no quick way of stepping through it. Instinct is all in Pursuit… good luck!

HIT & RUN

There's more than a touch of the Indiana Joneses to this one because the 24-foot bridge, suspended 12 feet in the air between the two towers, is being bombarded by four Gladiators, each with a four-foot diameter ball.

Two points is the meagre reward for each and every successful crossing – but once you're off, you're off! Hunter and Warrior are the Gladiators with the most successful strike rate, and sometimes have succeeded in a simultaneous hit by swinging from either side of the same platform in a 'flying Vee' shape. It's something of a cross between Swingshot and Suspension Bridge, and interestingly isn't on the list of any Gladiator's favourite event…yet!

Supertip: Concentrate on your peripheral vision – what's going on in the corner of your eye – but keep your gaze firmly ahead. And, whatever you do, *don't* be psyched out…

COBRA

BIRTHDATE 14 November 1960
BIRTHPLACE Jamaica
STAR SIGN Scorpio
HEIGHT 6ft
WEIGHT 15st
STATISTICS Chest 50in, waist 32in, thigh 26in, arm 18.5in

FAVOURITE EVENT
Hang Tough – 'I took to the rings like a fish to water!'

LEAST FAVOURITE EVENT
The Wall – 'It's hard on your biceps and tendons.'

FAVOURITE SPORTS
Boxing, kickboxing

OFF DUTY INTERESTS
When Cobra is not hanging out in the Danger Zone he enjoys watching the action men of the big screen, like Sylvester Stallone in the epic *Cliffhanger*. Then, after piling on the calories eating his favourite foods – pizza and cheesecake – what better way to burn them off than by going cycling?

❛ I think my strength is in being an all-rounder, whereas some of us are not too hot on certain events... I got quite good at Pyramid; I sussed it out, because they all take a bit of experimentation to work all the little nuances out when you're on there. ❜

❛ I eat sensibly 80 per cent of the time, and at weekends I throw caution to the wind and eat whatever I want. I call it the like diet...I eat whatever I like! ❜

BETCHA DIDN'T KNOW...

If it hadn't been for *Gladiators*, Cobra could be challenging the likes of Herbie Hide and Frank Bruno in the boxing ring. 'I wanted to get rich and famous somehow,' he says, 'so I started boxing. But I soon got fed up with having these big heavyweights punching me right in the face!' No such problems now...

❛ When you're in a contact game like Powerball, you've got to go in hard for self-preservation; if you go in for a tackle passively then you're going to get hurt. But when I'm taking them down I go, "Cor, your feet smell" – things like that! ❜

LIGHTNING

FAVOURITE EVENT
Hang Tough

LEAST FAVOURITE EVENT
Duel – 'I dislike it intensely! It's one on one and you're on a 12-foot platform, the spotlight's on you and everybody's looking at you.'

FAVOURITE SPORTS
Badminton, swimming, rollerblading

OFF DUTY INTERESTS
Lightning's television tastes centre firmly around comedy – namely Jennifer Saunders and Joanna Lumley in *Absolutely Fabulous*, along with *Roseanne* and *Barrymore*. One of her favourite movies is *The Bodyguard* starring Kevin Costner.

BIRTHDATE 25 December 1971
BIRTHPLACE Burntwood
STAR SIGN Capricorn
HEIGHT 5ft 7in
WEIGHT 9st 9lbs
STATISTICS 39-25-35

“The first year I ate everything and anything…I was one of the most powerful Gladiators out of the girls. Then I thought I didn't want to give that impression so I started to lose a little weight. This year I dieted right down and was really pleased…I looked pretty good.”

“It's a nice feeling knowing you make people happy. I'm proud to be a part of a sport that is exciting, competitive and entertaining. I just want to go on doing what I love – and knowing the audience loves it too!”

“Each year, *Gladiators* gets better and better. The new games have more body contact, which is good – it's better to watch and better to do. And even the speed games like Pursuit involve a lot of thinking, not just power or strength.”

BETCHA DIDN'T KNOW...

Lightning once competed with half of her Walkman headphones stuck in her hair when she got carried away listening to music backstage!

INTERNATIONAL GLADIATORS

FLYING THE FLAG – AND BEING A GLAD!

'They're fierce...they're ferocious...and they come from all four corners of the globe!' That's how the headlines announced *International Gladiators*, the ultimate fight of the fittest in which America, Russia and Finland joined Britain's very finest for a fight to the Finnish – make

International Gladiators - the guys!

that finish – at Birmingham's National Indoor Arena.

Our own Wolf, Trojan, Jet and Lightning played host to ten top-class colleagues, all determined to show that whatever we did they could do just as well...if not better. So while the Glads were brothers (and sisters) in arms, joining forces against contenders from all four countries, it's true to say that there was a certain amount of rivalry, not to mention national pride, at stake!

International Gladiators proved quite an experience, especially for the two Russians who'd never been to Britain before. But everyone found they spoke the same language – especially when they went on a paintball expedition together. 'We were all in camouflage gear,' recalls Hunter, 'and painted our faces. We had a lot of bruises, those paintballs don't half give you some gyp!'

Predictably, Wolf wasn't quite as impressed. 'The Americans were alright – for Americans. They were very brash but they weren't on a par with the British Gladiators... we're far better, and we're far better looking!'

For Hunter, the experience was nothing short of mind-blowing. 'I don't know where that's going to take us,' he says, 'but I think these international shows are really going to take the Gladiators up a step. I'm hoping we can maybe go to America or Finland and do some stuff over there!' Here's hoping...

INTERNATIONAL GLADIATORS: *WHO'S WHO*

Finland

Ultra-tough Terminator has 150 medals for cross-country skiing, and uses those powerful arms and upper body strength to 'hang tough' in his favourite event.

Blonde bombshell Flash combines jobs as a gym instructor and marketing student with a passion for Powerball.

Terminator - the Fin ready for action

Russia

At 6ft 7in and 18st 9lb, Spartak is the tallest and heaviest of the imports. Explosive enough to bust any Iron Curtain, his 55in chest and 21in biceps back up his slogan 'Victory at all costs'.

Dynamite is a Powerball specialist, just a stone lighter than his fellow Russian, but just as dynamic. His all-consuming passions? Bananas and classical composer Tchaikovsky!

America

Jazz - in style

Duel specialist Jazz hails from Houston, using her 12st 5lb to advantage, and off duty works in a chemical laboratory.

Ice claims she's clearly the coolest at Powerball, using her martial arts training to keep perfectly balanced.

Wall-climb expert Sky towers in the clouds at 6ft 3in – yet away from the Gladiatorial arena is a model and mother of two!

Nitro is the most agile of the American men. Tough too…he played football for the LA Rams.

Six foot two inch Sabre, who's a black belt at karate, has a 52in chest, a shaven head and an ultra-tough image.

Sabre and Jazz

TROJAN

FAVOURITE EVENT
Powerball – 'I just love that event – the tackling and the physical contact. It feels great to crush contenders…which is why I'm called "The Hitman".'

LEAST FAVOURITE EVENT
Tilt

FAVOURITE SPORTS
Bodybuilding

OFF DUTY INTERESTS
Trojan is very creative, listing drawing and writing among his interests – he even writes film scripts in his spare time. He also has a large collection of Walt Disney cartoon stills, including a *Lion King* one that cost £3000!

BIRTHDATE 25 February 1968
BIRTHPLACE Basingstoke
STAR SIGN Pisces
HEIGHT 6ft 2in
WEIGHT 17st
STATISTICS Chest 54in, waist 32in, thigh 28in, arm 20in

'*Gladiators* isn't just about being big, it's about being fast, agile, quick and lean.'

'I'll always remember going backstage and being congratulated after knocking my first two contenders off in Duel.'

BETCHA DIDN'T KNOW...

Globetrotting Trojan was living in Los Angeles and studying to become a professional bodybuilder when the call came to try out for *Gladiators*. 'The move back to England was the right one,' he smiles...and the rest is history!

'Life is not a rehearsal and I want to use everything I've got, every ounce of potential that I may have in every field.'

ZODIAC

BIRTHDATE 2 November 1965
BIRTHPLACE London
STAR SIGN Scorpio
HEIGHT 5ft 9in
WEIGHT 9st 12lbs
STATISTICS 38-26-35

FAVOURITE EVENT Skytrak – 'I love being suspended upside-down like a spider.'

LEAST FAVOURITE EVENT Pursuit – 'As soon as you start thinking about your contender or your next piece of apparatus, you've had it!'

FAVOURITE SPORTS Pole-vaulting

OFF DUTY INTERESTS This is one sporty lady! *Gladiators* aside, Zodiac loves athletics, walking, riding and learning new skills. And what better way to relax at the end of a hectic day than by listening to Dina Carroll and Julia Fordham while tucking into a bowl of Mexican tacos?

‘Being a Gladiator has given me more self-esteem and confidence. It does wonders knowing that out of thousands of applicants I was among those chosen to appear on one of LWT's most popular programmes.’

‘I have to be disciplined to make sure I get two or three hours training a day, otherwise you're going to be seriously shown up when it comes to television time. It's bye-bye social life!’

‘I do a lot of endurance and speed work, and I love being able to sprint to the top of the Pyramid – and tumbling down to the bottom!’

BETCHA DIDN'T KNOW...

Zodiac was recruited to the *Gladiators*' ranks in 1993 at only two weeks notice – an experience she found quite breathtaking. 'I was so intent on trying to impress the others and be part of the team,' she admits. Now though, she's an established favourite!

SARACEN

BIRTHDATE 30 August 1963
BIRTHPLACE London
STAR SIGN Virgo
HEIGHT 6ft 3in
WEIGHT 17st 7lbs
STATISTICS Chest 46in, bicep 18.5in, thigh 26.5in

FAVOURITE EVENT
Hang Tough – 'Once you start swinging, you're hooked!'

LEAST FAVOURITE EVENT
None: this fearless fella claims to enjoy them all!

FAVOURITE SPORTS
Bodybuilding

OFF DUTY INTERESTS
Bodybuilding – this is one Gladiator who seems to have a one-track mind…though he will admit to being partial to a little bit of soul music when he's in need of rest and relaxation.

"I don't mind being recognised, but I couldn't take being mobbed like *The Beatles* were at airports. You can't do a thing then, can you? You can't even go in Tesco's!"

"We are getting tougher contenders coming along. But people don't realise fitness is an overall thing. It's strength and endurance and stamina, the whole package."

"Contenders always seem to start off too quickly on the Eliminator. Then when they come down to the last crucial part, the travelator, they can't do it. The mind goes – and once the mind goes, the body follows!"

BETCHA DIDN'T KNOW...

Saracen combined his job as a professional firefighter with TV work as an extra. The most famous person he ever met was Frank Bruno when he was playing the boxer's double in a programme about his life.

SCORPIO

FAVOURITE EVENT
Powerball – 'Taking a flying leap and throwing your whole bodyweight down is quite extraordinary.'

LEAST FAVOURITE EVENT
Atlaspheres – 'I don't like to be caged.'

FAVOURITE SPORTS
Gymnastics, athletics

OFF DUTY INTERESTS
Reading aside, sci-fi fan Scorpio likes nothing better than to spend time with her daughter Emily, who's also a mad-keen athlete. When the day's all but over, she settles down with her husband in front of the T.V. to watch a film.

BIRTHDATE 15 March 1965
BIRTHPLACE Isle Of Man
STAR SIGN Pisces
HEIGHT 5ft 9in
WEIGHT 10st
STATISTICS 40-24-35

"I'm very determined, very fixed and very focussed in one direction. The second time I ever did The Wall, I did it faster than the guy who taught me to climb it!"

"I always wish I'd done better because I've got a competitive nature, so obviously I want to win!"

"I'm one of those people who just has to train in the mornings - it's just my body clock. But to relax, I'm an avid reader - you would not believe my science fiction collection!"

BETCHA DIDN'T KNOW...

When the curtain finally comes down on her career as a Gladiator, Scorpio wants to stay in front of the cameras! Eventually, she would like to be a TV presenter – either that, or play the lead in a sword and sorcery movie.

WARRIOR

BIRTHDATE 30 December 1960
BIRTHPLACE St Helens
STAR SIGN Capricorn
HEIGHT 6ft 5in
WEIGHT 20st 10lbs
STATISTICS Chest 56in, waist 38in, arm 22in, thigh 31in

FAVOURITE EVENT
Powerball – 'My height and weight are my obvious strengths and I use them to my advantage.'

LEAST FAVOURITE EVENT
Hang Tough

FAVOURITE SPORTS
Soccer, rugby, golf.

OFF DUTY INTERESTS
You might not be able to picture Warrior teeing off, but golf is one of his consuming passions. So is eating out, though he confesses he's no gourmet – his favourite food is Kentucky Fried Chicken.

‘I was given the name Warrior in the beginning, because I was the biggest Gladiator. I just trundle on, do my job and get off – and the job's well done, like a warrior of old I suppose.’

‘It's great to see the smile and enjoyment you bring to millions of children. Even after three years, you wonder why they want your autograph. A couple of years ago I was just a bodybuilder, nobody!’

‘I didn't imagine *Gladiators* would be as successful as it has been…but thank God it has! They said it would change our lives and I wasn't really ready – but it's a good life and a very rewarding one.’

BETCHA DIDN'T KNOW...

Warrior's been training with Tranmere's Eire international footballer John Aldridge to help him lose bulk and cope with the newer games – two hours a day, five days a week!

Are You Ready For The GLADIATORS™ CHALLENGE?

These 20 testing questions will find out what you really know about Britain's toughest televised sports challenge and the people who play it. Each question has three possible answers: simply choose one, then refer to the answers to see how you rate.

"Contenders ready?"

1 Which Gladiator starred as Fairy Bowbells in the panto Dick Whittington?
a Panther
b Falcon
c Zodiac

2 Which of these footballers has not starred in *Celebrity Gladiators*?
a Mark Bosnich
b Ian Rush
c Vinny Jones

3 Which famous transport system invited Panther and Trojan to travel on its first journey?
a Concorde London-New York
b The Space Shuttle
c The Channel Tunnel

4 Which Gladiator was the British women's pole-vaulting champion when she became a Gladiator?
a Jet
b Zodiac
c Nightshade

5 How long must contenders stay on The Wall to claim five points?
a 1 minute
b 90 seconds
c 45 seconds

6 How many rings are there in the Hang Tough zone?
a 6
b 60
c 166

7 Which Gladiator lost a stone for the third series of *Gladiators* so he could improve his agility – but lost none of his strength?
a Hunter
b Saracen
c Wolf

8 What happy event happened to *Gladiators* co-host Ulrika Jonsson at the end of the third series?
a She got married
b She had a baby boy
c She was voted TV's 'rear of the year'

9 What is Trojan's nickname due to his amazing skill in Powerball?
a The Terminator
b The Hitman
c The Outsider

10 Who was the first Gladiator to have a video made about her?
a Scorpio
b Nightshade
c Jet

11 Which football club signed co-host John Fashanu in the summer of 1994?
a Wimbledon
b Aston Villa
c Liverpool

12 Which Gladiator carries the logo of an ancient sword on his outfit?
a Trojan
b Saracen
c Shadow

13 In which city's Indoor Arena is *Gladiators* filmed?
a London
b Manchester
c Birmingham

14 Which Gladiator is a three-time Olympic athlete?
a Nightshade
b Warrior
c Scorpio

15 In Powerball, how many baskets are there?
a Four
b Five
c Six

16 Which Gladiator was disturbed in her bathroom by *The Big Breakfast*'s Keith Chegwin?
a Lightning
b Falcon
c Jet

17 What is the first challenge facing contenders in the Eliminator?
a Cargo net
b Four hurdles

c Rope climb

18 Which Gladiator paints her initial on her arm to look like a tattoo?
a Lightning
b Zodiac
c Falcon

19 Which event involves a tug of war between Gladiator and contender?
a Atlaspheres
b Duel
c Tilt

20 Which Gladiator combined bodybuilding with a successful modelling career?
a Wolf
b Falcon
c Scorpio

THE ANSWERS

1 b, 2 b, 3 c, 4 b, 5 a, 6 b, 7 a, 8 b, 9 b, 10 c, 11 b, 12 b, 13 c, 14 a, 15 b, 16 a, 17 b, 18 b, 19 c, 20 c.

HOW YOU SCORED

17-20
You're in the Gladiator class when it comes to mental agility – if you've got the physique to go with it, the sky's the limit!

11-16
Not bad…but you got caught out in the Eliminator! Hang Tough, keep watching and you could just make a comeback.

5-10
You need to get some serious training under your belt! Read the rest of this book and come back next year.

UNDER 5
Call yourself a contender? Get outta here before we send the Wolfman round!

NIGHTSHADE

BIRTHDATE 14 November 1960
BIRTHPLACE Jamaica
STAR SIGN Scorpio
HEIGHT 6ft
WEIGHT 11st
STATISTICS 36-27-39

FAVOURITE EVENT Pyramid – 'You get a bit of everything, you can have a good tussle with the contender, you can use tactics and you have to recover well. It also helps if you're fast off the mark.'

LEAST FAVOURITE EVENT Hit & Run – 'I like more active events, and swinging a ball doesn't really do much for me…'

FAVOURITE SPORTS Athletics, climbing, Tai Kwon-Do

OFF DUTY INTERESTS Home-lovin' Nightshade enjoys spending time with her friends and family. When she ventures out, she can often be found at the cinema watching action movies like *Demolition Man*.

“I thoroughly enjoyed Powerball. I'm better at tackling now, I've been practising and I've had help from some of the best rugby players in the country.”

“I don't get very excited about weight problems and diet because I've known too many friends who have developed eating disorders and get totally paranoid about their food – so I don't like to go over the top. Everything in moderation…”

“Usually if you get very angry you don't perform so well, so it's something I try to avoid. The only time I get wound up is if someone is incredibly rude to me…I'll definitely make sure they know I'm annoyed!”

BETCHA DIDN'T KNOW…

Apart from being the tallest female Gladiator at 6 foot, Nightshade is well equipped in the brains department too! She once studied law and sociology.

TM